Momma, I Wanna be Light-skinned:

My Journey to Acceptance

Rhonda R. Bennett

To Felencia,

Thanks so much for walking into my office when you did! You have been an inspiration... more than you know!

R Bennett

Momma, I Wanna be Light-skinned

Cover design and Layout by Nailah Lawrence
Nailahrenaedesigns.com

Author photo provided by Khayla Williams Photography

ISBN-13:978-1508733294
ISBN-10:1508733295

This book is dedicated to my wonderful husband Kevin, and two amazing sons, Ethan and Caleb.

Contents

Acknowledgements…………………………………………7

Foreword…………………………………………10

Preface…………………………………………14

Introduction…………………………………………18

Age of Innocence…………………………………………20

Big Honey…………………………………………22

Home Life…………………………………………26

Shielded…………………………………………29

Eyes Wide Shut…………………………………………33

Innocence Betrayed…………………………………………38

So Long/Farewell…………………………………………44

My Best Friend…………………………………………46

Launch Prep 101…………………………………………49

Showtime…………………………………………52

No More Daddy's Little Girl…………………………………………54

Secret from the Bayou…………………………………………60

From Pain to Anger…………………………………………64

Rude Awakening…………………………………………68

Anger Management……………………………....72

Finding My Place…………………...………….74

Hungry for Validation…………………………...77

Withdrawn…………………………….…………80

My Kin…………………………………………..81

Spirit Fingers………………………………….84

She's Your Queen to Be…………………………86

I'll Show You…………………………………..90

Big Fish…………………………………………95

Courage to Move………………………………98

My New Home……………………………….100

The "Crab" Year………………………….....102

Him……………………………………………104

Turn for the Worse……………………….......106

The Morning After……………………………111

Whenever, Wherever, Whatever……………….113

The Encounter…………………………………111

The Encounter Part 2…………………...……..114

In the Meantime………………………………116

I See the Light...118

The Awakening...121

Left without Answers..................................127

Love the Hurt Away.............................……133

My Intended..135

Back Down Memory Lane..............................139

The Hard Truth..142

The Process..143

Step by Step..145

Press Delete..148

Uniquely You...150

My Resolve...152

About the Author..162

Acknowledgments

To the one who loved me first, it's only in You that I live, move, and have my being. Thank you God for loving me when I didn't love myself. Thank you for guiding me through this journey to wholeness. Though I tried to escape the process many times, You held me close and reminded me of Your word over my life. I pray that You are pleased with me.

To my husband, my intended blessing, my biggest supporter, my shoulder to cry on, my gift that keeps on giving, and my best friend, Kevin. Thank you for the gentle nudging compelling me to hurry up and finish this book. Thank you for believing in me and being a voice of hope during the many times I wanted to give up. Thank you for giving me the time and space to figure things out. I know it was a sacrifice. I will forever be grateful to you for your selfless support. I hope I made you proud. I love you.

To Ethan and Caleb...you are my why! You motivate me to be a better mommy. I desire for you to pursue your dreams without limitations. You can and will accomplish great things. Thank you for being two of the most wonderful sons for whom a mother could ask. I love you.

Mom, words could never describe how much I appreciate the sacrifice you made to ensure that I had all I needed and most of what I wanted. You have been the wind beneath my wings. You encouraged me to soar above the clouds of doubt and dare to achieve all that I desired. Thank you for telling me I could even when I thought I couldn't. You continue to inspire me. I love you.

Toya, thank you for being obedient in your path that our paths might cross. You are one of the greatest friends I've ever known. I'm excited to see where God takes us next! Love you!

Nailah, you are the best. Thank you for helping me fulfill my vision. You answered every email, returned every call, and worked tirelessly on my book design. You are my graphic artist for life.

To all of my family and friends who walked with me through this process. Thank you for your words of reassurance along this journey. Thank you for scolding me when I lost focus. Thank you for holding me accountable. I love you all!

To my readers…this is for you. Thank you for picking up this book and reading about some of my experiences. My hope is that you find yourself somewhere in my story. I hope to inspire you to tell your story and begin healing. You are worth it! I am cheering for you!

Foreword

"Sticks and stones may break my bones, but words will never harm me!" As popular as those words are among children around the world, Rhonda Bennett learned first-hand the lack of truth contained within them. Words can and often times do hurt us. The words we speak as well as the words we internalize from others have the ability to positively or negatively affect us for a lifetime. This is especially true when those words are spoken by the individuals we love the most.

In the book, "Momma I Wanna be Light-Skinned: My Journey to Acceptance," Rhonda Bennett chronicles her journey from being an innocent girl full of self-confidence to the moment her innocence was stripped, to becoming a woman who just recently became comfortable in her own skin. Although the overarching theme of this book is about her personal battle to accept that her black is beautiful, there are underlying themes contained within the pages of this book.

Because of the racism that has plagued America and in this particular case, the state of Alabama, many of its citizens of color have concluded that the historical racist viewpoint that "white is right" has truth to it. That mentality is addressed in this book.

Erroneous beliefs such as "white is right" have perpetuated in the lives of many African-Americans from generation to generation. In an attempt to be proactive in the well-being of her future great-grandchildren, Rhonda's grand-mother spoke what she believed to be words of wisdom that would propel Rhonda to be proactive in assuring that her children have their fair share of opportunities in America. What she didn't know is that those words would become the catalyst of Rhonda's battle with negative self-images. The words that parents speak over their children have great influence.

Actions speak louder than words. No matter how much a person says that a particular thing is their preference, if that person is always pursuing the exact opposite, their real preference becomes abundantly clear. In this case, the two men Rhonda admired the most provided evidence of a preference that chipped away at her already deteriorating self-image. Studies show that 90% of all women want to change at least one thing about their physical appearance. The causes mentioned range from sexual objectification to media pressure to internalized negative comments. In this book, Rhonda speaks as one of the 90% and gives readers a glimpse into the real life of a woman who overcame the battle of low self-esteem birthed from a negative self-image.

How could the Campus Queen of one of U.S. News top 50 HBCU's be featured in an edition of

Ebony Magazine and yet not believe that her exterior is just as beautiful as the interior it houses?

Journey through these poignant forty-five chapters and not only experience Rhonda's victory, but experience your own.

~Romel Gibson~

Campus Life Director, Tuscaloosa Youth for Christ

Youth Pastor, Plum Grove Baptist Church

Preface

Have you ever been in such a low place that you had to do a double take and ask yourself, "How did I get here?" This is what I asked myself 5 years ago. I had just given birth to my second son. In the midst of feeling all of the emotions that come with the birth of a new baby, one sentiment echoed the loudest. Depression! I wasn't new to this feeling. In fact, it was eerily familiar.

I looked down at my newborn and didn't see myself. He was beautiful and fair-skinned with curly locks. I beamed with joy because God had given me what I prayed for, another boy. Though my first born was just as handsome and fair-skinned with curly hair and dimples, I didn't have the overwhelming sense of guilt that I had this time. My second pregnancy was so different. I thought I was having a girl. I was in fear of that probability for half of my pregnancy. The thought of bringing a girl into this world who would no doubt look like me, terrified me! Imagine the relief I felt after the doctor shouted "it's a boy!" I was ecstatic! But now meeting this baby that I prayed for was bitter-sweet. The very words that left me ecstatic now left me feeling ashamed.

How did I get here? When did I began to hate myself? I couldn't have loved myself because I didn't even want my child to look like me. Why? More importantly, why was I feeling this way now? I desperately needed answers.

One day as I was feeding my son, I had a memory of the moment that set me on the path to self-hatred. It answered my question. A seed had been sown during my childhood. It was buried so deep in my subconscious that I'd forgotten about it until now. That seed slowly sprouted and produced fruit in different seasons of my life. As I delve more into how I became who I am, I noticed patterns that stemmed from that pivotal moment; patterns of low self-esteem, insufficiency, and the need for validation from those around me. Those patterns ultimately guided me in every decision I made. A lot of which were bad. I gradually connected the dots. I realized that my life was a counterfeit, fashioned by an idea enrooted by another person.

It's amazing how we live our lives based on the negative opinions of others. This was indeed my life and I needed to be healed from the life that was created for me.

I sought refuge in my journal. Writing has given me the courage to confront the very thing I'd been running from my entire life---myself. As I write, I keep in mind that there's a little girl who lacks the confidence to pursue her dreams; an elderly woman who wishes she could have pushed passed the prohibitions of her peers to realize her full potential; a woman who's just like me, waking up from the anesthesia of words spoken that kept her sedated just long enough to make her believe that mediocrity was her destiny. Now awake, I see greatness was always attainable.

It is my intention to rescue you. Wherever you may be on the spectrum, realize today that you have the power to create the next moments in your life. Your perspective is the only one that matters.

Introduction

I exhibited strength when everything about me was weak. My struggle was real to me. I searched for identity. I searched for acceptance. I was so desperate for validation that I welcomed the temporary fix of a stranger's love. At least it gave me a chance to escape my inner torture; if only for a moment. I was on the hunt for something. I know now that I was looking for my value, my purpose. Unfortunately, those two virtues wouldn't be realized until years later.

Still the more pressing question remained. Was I destined to live a life full of disappointment, rejection, anger, and distrust? I wasted so much time trying to fit the mold and be accepted. Playing the "it" game in life. Longing to be tagged and hear those magic words, "You're it! It's your turn!" There I stood on the sidelines surrounded by my own poisonous thoughts. The more I thought, the more my standing turned into sinking. Soon I was drowning in the ocean of lies told to me by others that I ultimately believed. I cried out for someone to throw me a lifeline.

"Help me! I don't want to be like this anymore!"

Somewhere in the depth of my despair, words that I'd heard many times before but never fully believed, began to pierce the very core of my spirit. They resounded in my soul and echoed in my ear.

"You were fearfully and wonderfully made."

I found comfort and tranquility in those words.

That was the beginning of my healing.

This is my story. This is my journey to acceptance.

Chapter One

Age of innocence

She always treated me differently. I remember feeling as though she never wanted me around. At the time, it didn't really matter to me. I liked being around her. She had a dry sense of humor, though quite funny at times. Her house was filled with the sounds of music and laughter. I can still smell the aroma of freshly baked tea cakes and peppermint. I enjoyed most of our visits; except when she wanted me to help clean her house. She would call just about every Saturday and ask my mom, "Can Rhonda come over and help me clean the house?"

I would contend with mom and question, "Why do I have to go? I don't live there!" Mom would squint her eyes and reply, "You're going."

I didn't care about cleaning. I hated going because I would end up doing most of the work. At least it seemed that way to me! This was the source of my contention. My cousin and two of my uncles lived with her as well. She really didn't need me. I guess she figured she could make me do anything since I was the baby.

What puzzled me was the fact that my mother would take me over there knowing what would happen. I guess she figured she didn't have a choice; realizing she needed a babysitter for those times she wanted to go to the dog track. I could always stay there and pay by providing sanitation services.

Chapter 2

Big Honey

Big Honey is what they called her. She was about 5'10" with golden skin, high cheek bones, red silky hair and an attitude to match. I guess the name Big Honey was appropriate.

She was a fox back in her day, or so I heard. Even in her seasoned age, she still had a bit of sassiness in her walk. She would tip across the room in her pumps full of confidence. Her head was always held high. I wanted to be like her, look like her.

I loved her hair! It was smooth and straight; a stark difference from my nappy hair. I loved touching her hair.

"Grandma, can I comb your hair?" I'd eagerly ask. Hesitantly, she'd reply, "Yeah, I guess so. Bring the grease too."

She loved having her scalp scratched and greased. Big Honey used to keep Blue Magic Hair Dress on her dresser in the bedroom. I liked going in her bedroom. It smelled of perfume and gum. I would take my time getting the comb and grease just so I could sneak a piece of gum and peek at her dresses and hats. She loved to dress up, smell good, and chew gum! Tresor was the scent of choice and Freedent was the gum of choice.

I would get so lost in the aroma of her sweet perfume and the satisfaction of chewing a piece of minty gum that I would forget why I'd gone into her room. Soon that mature voice would yell from the living room to remind me, "Hurry up and get out of my room!"

"I couldn't find the comb grandma", I'd say, running back to the living room. I didn't dare tell her what I was really doing, though I'm sure she smelled the gum on my breath.

She would stretch out on the couch and tilt her head back. Her hair seemed to flow over the arm of the couch. I gently combed her finely textured hair and watched the waves form throughout the sea of red strands. I would brush her hair after applying the grease to her scalp. The soft stroke of the bristles against her head would put her to sleep every time. One day, after she had fallen asleep, I decided that I wanted to see what her hair looked like curly. I knew she would be excited to have a new hair style. I was around seven years old at the time and didn't really know any better. So, I naively grabbed the wide tooth comb that I used to scratch her scalp and proceeded to roll her hair with the comb. I slowly released the comb. Her hair looked nice, so I continued. The next time I attempted a spiral curl. I rolled the comb under like before, but this time, I twisted the comb and rolled it to one side. I even let the comb sit in her hair to set the curl like a curling iron. I couldn't wait to see the look on her face when she saw her new hairdo. I was so excited! To my surprise, her hair did not turn out the way I expected. In fact, it didn't immediately come out of the comb. Her hair was tangled. As I desperately tried to free granny's hair from the comb, it hit me. I would have to wake her. I cried a little before I called her name. After I woke her, I cried a lot. She was so mad at me. I felt that whipping for days! Needless to say, it would be years before I could touch her again. I did however, continue my Saturday morning routine. I was accustomed to it by now.

Chapter Three

Home Life

Saturday mornings in my house consisted of early morning cartoons, a big bowl of cereal, and of course, hours of cleaning. My mom was a stickler for a clean house; no dishes in the sink, swept and mopped floors. There was a place for everything and everything had a place. We didn't live in a mansion, but what we had was nice and always clean.

I was the last child in the house by age seven, so I quickly became acclimated to mopping floors, cleaning bathrooms, and taking out the trash. I was mowing the lawn by age nine. I was pretty good at it too! I was so good that my dad bought a riding mower for me. My first time driving! I treated it like a car! It had a clutch too! I was driving a stick shift! I was so excited! Oh my goodness! I loved it!

I spent a lot of time outside under the hot sun. I loved to feel the warm sun against my face. My mom didn't like it though. However, it wasn't the health aspect that bothered her. She was concerned about my complexion. She complained to my dad about having me outside in the middle of the day. Though it wasn't the hottest time of day, the sun was still bright, and mom would scold dad and say, "Rhonda's getting darker from being outside in the sun."

Dad would wave her off and say, "She'll be alright!"

Sure enough, my complexion would return to normal after a few hours. Nevertheless, mom thought I was getting darker. I couldn't even play outside for a lengthy amount of time. I would run out of the house to meet my friends and she would yell to me, "Don't be in the sun too long…make sure you find some shade, and be back in this house before the street lights come on!" I didn't pay much attention to the part about the sun; but she was serious about the street lights.

I remember one time, I thought I'd see if my mom really watched the street lights come on, so I stayed out a little longer. I saw the glow of light above me increase as the sun dimmed around me. All of a sudden, I heard my mom's voice echoing down the street! "Rhonda!"

Her voice sounded as if it was reaching out to grab me. I think she knew the schedule for the lights. I believe she was standing at the door, watching the light, and waiting on me at the same time. She must have had her car keys in her hand as well, because shortly after I heard my name, I saw her car coming down the street. I got an earful that night.

It's funny now, but it wasn't then.

Chapter Four

Shielded

I understand now that my mom was just trying to protect me. She did her best to shield me from hurt and disappointment. She wanted me to focus on my talent. I could sing back then. I even played the piano. My mom was my biggest cheerleader. She made sure I was in every talent show, city event, or anything that would show the world that her baby could sing. We lived in a small town, so most of the people knew who I was from seeing me perform. Even if they didn't know me, they knew my mom and thought twice about telling her no.

I saw the effort and sacrifice that she made to further my passion. She instilled in me, confidence and pride that couldn't be broken, or so I thought! Although I had a supportive mom, I still had struggles with peer acceptance. Who didn't at nine years old? I had a few friends that I would talk to everyday or as much as a fourth grader could and they were great! Regrettably, the ones who were loudest in my ear were those who found pleasure in talking negatively about me.

I never told my mom about my problem with bullies or the hurtful names I was subjected to on a daily basis. She would have tried to handle it, and that would have made things worse and given my peers yet another reason to dislike me.

My mom was a teacher. She travelled thirty minutes to a small town to teach Language Arts at a high school. I attended the elementary school in that town. I preferred to attend school back home, but I imagine having me in close proximity kept her mind at ease. I wished I could ride the bus to school with my neighborhood friends.

My town was awesome. It was filled with historical treasures. Penned by one as "the pride of the swift growing south," many pay homage to the small town that has had such a huge impact; from the "Tails" that flew proudly across the skies leaving streaks of red by which we remember their sacrifice; to the inventor who discovered so many uses for the peanut that even today, the most practical invention remains the better half of the perfect marriage of peanut butter and jelly; to the institute that opened its doors, despite adversity, to future ministers, nurses, and teachers, and has advanced to a university of higher learning; developing thousands of biologists, doctors, and engineers. Yes, my town was always a topic of discussion during Black History Month. I guess I can understand why my peers resented me, at least during the month of February.

What they didn't know was beneath the hoarded wealth of my town, was an ever present, ever growing complexion divide that resonated between the haves and the have not's…the dark-skinned and the lighter-than skinned. It separated the players on the field from the water boys. It preferred those being served over the servants. Favor was given to those who had earned the right to be in the spotlight for merely having the acceptable color properties of the time. It shunned those whose hue was too dark to be desired. Yes, my town had an undeniable contribution to our nation's story of triumph, but between the pages of the story, rested the dissension within our own race. I experienced it firsthand; primarily name calling by peers: "blacky", "tar baby", "smut", and "ashes", just to name a few. I tried to blow it off. I told myself they're just goofing around. They don't really mean it. Do they?

Chapter Five

Eyes Wide Shut

I didn't pay much attention to my complexion before the fourth grade. I suppose I was one of the darker kids in the class, but I didn't notice the difference. Most of us, with the exception of a few, shared the same hue.

Fourth grade was brutal. My physical appearance was scrutinized every day. Maybe the aforementioned facts about my hometown fueled the name calling; or maybe it was the notion that dark-skin was synonymous with ugly. Perhaps the other kids treated me like they were being treated. I don't really know. Truth is, most of the girls in movies, music videos or commercials were light-skinned with long hair. Nonetheless, I was fed up with the constant taunting, and I wanted to put an end to it. It was time for me to defend myself.

One day, as fate would have it, the culmination of all the ridicule and embarrassing jokes ended with two bloody noses and a stained, turquoise jump suit. I'd had enough. The two of us were sent to the office and given a paddling by our principal with the "enforcer". The "enforcer" was a 4x4 piece of wood, wrapped in several layers of masking tape. The tape, we were told, was there to prevent splinters. Consequently, it managed to increase the sting of the paddle.

The principal knew of my growing frustration. I'd talked to him several times before concerning the name calling. He quickly intervened. My teacher was instructed to excuse me from class after I completed my assignment. I would go the office and help the secretary staple papers or fill the mail slots. The time in the office helped me avoid the imminent conflict. However, this time, I was confronted while the teacher was out of class. I had two options: continue to run or fight. I chose to fight.

The principal was surprised. I think he was proud of me. He delivered seven hard whacks to the instigator's backside but only gave me three. I knew then, he was happy that I defended myself. He dismissed the other girl but kept me in the office.

He knew something else had transpired to send me over the edge. He saw my nonchalant attitude, and heard my snappy answers. With a concerned look and softness in his voice, he asked, "What really happened?"

I couldn't tell him the whole truth.

"I hate her and I'm tired of being talked about," I calmly replied.

 I saw the confusion in his eyes. He heard the conviction in my voice. He knew there was more.

"Hate," he questioned, "That's a strong word for a little girl." "That's how I feel", I snapped.

He knew better. I didn't sound like the happy girl he talked to just a few days prior. He pressed me for answers but I refused to repeat those words spoken to me last night. I was afraid that I might believe them.

My innocence betrayed me the night before. She, along with others, made me believe for nine years that those closest to me would love and protect me unconditionally. She made me believe that I could expect different from those whose blood ran through my veins. Innocence had me blinded by birthday and Christmas gifts, hugs, kisses on the cheek, and words of love. She made me believe in those things and then ripped the veil of illusion to expose the harsh truth of reality. Why give me a false sense of self? I was supposed to feel secure.

Well I didn't anymore!

Chapter Six

Innocence Betrayed

My mother had gone to the grocery store for grandma and left me at her house for a short while. The house was humid due to the heat and air conditioner's synchronized settings. My skin felt sticky. My body didn't know whether to be hot or cold. I was uncomfortable. In an attempt to escape the expanding thermal pressure, I lay down on the floor to cool off. I was watching TV. I don't remember much else from that night or the events that led up to what happened next. However, the image I'll never forget is my grandma's face as she looked down at me. Her eyes peered over the top of her glasses as she carefully picked up her spit cup. She pursed her lips and released the liquid that had accumulated from the tobacco, and slowly placed the cup on the floor. She was watching me. She began talking to me, but I had no idea what she was saying. I was distracted by the show on TV. Perhaps she was asking me to get the hair grease and comb since I was in her good graces again. She must have noticed the blank expression on my face because she yelled out, "Rhonda! Did you hear me?" I was jolted by her stern voice.

"No." I said. "Did you ask me to get your comb?" I said expectantly.

"No," she retorted. "I said you need to marry someone white or high-yella if you want your children to have a chance in this world."

I sat there for a moment trying to process what she said. "Did I hear her correctly," I thought to myself.

I must have had a puzzled look on my face because she quickly repeated herself.

"If you want to have children, make sure you marry someone white or high-yella if you want them to have a chance!"

I heard her loud and clear this time. I was confused. What was she talking about, and more importantly, why would she say that to me?

I massaged my forehead trying to wrap my innocent mind around what her words meant. Was she implying that I was too dark-skin to make it in the world? Was she warning me or was she being mean to me like the kids in my class? Question after question formed in my head. Too afraid to ask her for answers, I put my head down and waited on an explanation or at the least, consolation. Neither came. My confidence and pride escaped me in that moment, and self-doubt rushed in and took their place. In those few minutes, I second guessed everything that my mother told me:

"I was pretty."

Lie!

"I could be anything, do anything, and go anywhere I want to go in life."

Lie! Lie! Lie! All lies!

How could I believe my mom, when her own mother just told me the opposite? Did my mother fear the same fate for me? Is that why she desperately pursued opportunities that would allow my talent to outshine my potential handicap?

Why was this happening? Why now?

I was nine years old.

It seemed like hours had passed before my mom arrived. Upon leaving, my grandma hugged me and said, "See you Saturday." She acted as though nothing had happened. My arms remained at my side.

I was quiet on the way home. Mom asked if anything had happened at grandma's house.

"Nothing really," I simply stated. Mom wasn't sure of my answer so she asked if I was sure. I told her yes and continued to gaze out the window into the black night.

I couldn't sleep! I wanted to talk to my mom but I didn't know what to say. Would she even believe me, or worse would she share the same sentiments as her mother?

Did it really happen, or was I so poisoned by the words spoken to me on a daily basis by my peers, that I imagined my beautiful, red-boned grandma utter the same words? Surely not! She didn't call me names or make fun of my complexion. She said I needed to marry a white man or "high-yella" black man if I wanted my kids to have a chance in the world.

My mother married my father, a dark man, and I look just like him. Did grandma tell my mom the same thing she told me? Did she dislike my dad and take her frustration out on me? So many questions left unanswered. My innocence was gone. I had been exposed to a betrayal that a nine year old shouldn't have experienced. I was made aware of an idea that changed my outlook on life;

the idea of being less than. I was less than. The person I thought I knew, no longer existed. She was a stranger, and so was I.

Regrettably, evidence of my grandmother's words manifested two times before my 10th birthday.

Chapter Seven

So Long! Farewell!

After the fight at school, I begged my mom to transfer me to a school in our hometown. I knew things would be better! She didn't like the idea at first. The thought of being thirty minutes away from me versus the current five minutes, petrified her. She wanted to ensure my safety, but she could only do that if she was right next to me. Mom had no idea of what I had already experienced. Furthermore, she couldn't prevent future conflicts. Somehow, I convinced mom to let me attend school at home. Though I'd have to wait a few months before the transition, I was eager to tell my classmates about my upcoming departure. Some of my peers took that time to taunt me and pick a few more fights, but I was fine. I knew that I would be leaving soon and would never see some of them again.

Chapter Eight

My Best Friend

In spite of the pain that I was experiencing in my life, I found joy in seeing my mom accomplish her dreams.

She started a venture that was sure to put us in the presence of great people. It was a magazine entitled, "La Fleur de Lis". It's a French expression, defined as "the flower of the lily". It sounded pretty. I think she chose that name out of her new fondness for the city of New Orleans. The Fleur de Lis is a symbol there. We were introduced to the "Big Easy" by way of my brother. He went to college there. I remember the ride to New Orleans. It was the longest 5 hours of my life. I couldn't grasp the thought of leaving my brother in a strange place.

He, like my mother, was the other powerful voice in my ear telling me I was pretty as pretty could be. We were inseparable. Though there's a 10 year age difference between us, he still included me in just about every aspect of his life; even his relationships.

We entered a dance contest his junior year of high school. We worked on a routine for weeks. We should have won! I don't remember the song we danced to, but it was one of the most memorable moments we shared.

He was a star basketball player in high school. We attended every home game, and travelled to most away games. He was consistently honored for his success on and off the court. He was the best! My brother made me feel secure. I didn't doubt his love for me.

We dropped him off at college shortly after my eighth birthday. He hugged and kissed me and told me he would call me often and visit as much as he could. I cried all the way home. I missed him so much. Mom missed him too. I think the idea of the magazine was birthed out of her need to fill the void caused by his absence. She needed a new undertaking.

Chapter Nine

Launch Prep 101

Mom was a creative and sharp woman. She designed magazine layouts, hired models and photographers. She rallied the help of clothing stores to make her vision a reality. Everything was going according to plan! Though months of preparation were ahead, she was determined to see it through.

Our first photo shoot was amazing. I was a model! The props and lighting were similar to a movie set. The next step was showcase. Since the magazine launch was scheduled for August, the showcase would be in July. It would offer potential customers a peek of what to expect in the magazine.

With clipboard in hand, mom meticulously marked off each item for the show: Choreography?

Check.

Music?

Check.

Wardrobe?

Check. It was sure to be amazing.

The excitement was building. Everything was moving so fast that I'd forgotten about the dysfunction in my life. I was reminded after I saw my pictures from the photo shoot. They looked awful. The lamp must have been turned off because all of my frames were too dark. I hated the pictures. I didn't want to be in the showcase anymore. I was afraid someone else might say the same thing grandma said. What if someone yelled out while I was on stage, "I can't see her…turn on the lights"? I couldn't take that chance. I only wanted to help behind the scenes. Mom convinced me that I would be beautiful, so I pressed on in spite of my fears.

Chapter Ten

Showtime

Opening night was magical! It was the manifestation of months of drafting designs, recruiting models, photo shoots and late night rehearsals. I was so proud of my mom.

She was beautiful in her black A-lined, floor length skirt, and metallic gold, swoop necked blouse. The glow of pride that beamed from her face was priceless. In that moment, my grandmother's words didn't matter. I truly believed I could accomplish anything. I witnessed my mom's perseverance result in success. The models looked amazing; the dancers were flawless.

Mom was praised for her vision and validated in her success. Her magazine was the start of a new life for us. I knew that I would remember that night forever. Regrettably, I would remember it for all the wrong reasons. I didn't know that betrayal lurked in the shadows, waiting to deliver a harsh blow.

Chapter Eleven

No More Daddy's Little Girl

Mom and I talked about our exciting night. We wished it could go on, but it was late and I needed to go to sleep. I took a shower, put on my pajamas and got into bed. I whispered the Lord's Prayer and fell asleep.

I was a sound sleeper. It was hard to wake me up. Once, I slept through a terrible storm. I recall waking up the next morning with no electricity. My parents were outside assessing the damage. Shingles were missing off the roof, and the screen door was blown off by strong winds. Mom and dad concluded that a tornado had touched down near our house. Mom expressed her frustration with attempting to wake me, but I wouldn't budge. She just prayed while I slept. I could sleep through anything.

But tonight was different.

I was violently awakened to the sounds of a woman screaming. My heart began to pound rapidly. I was frozen in my bed. I remained still for a few seconds just to make sure I wasn't dreaming. Fear overtook me. I heard it again. I wasn't dreaming. I jumped up and peeked down the hall. It was dark. I didn't see anyone, but the screams grew louder. I heard a sound I didn't recognize, but with soon I'd become acquainted. I turned on the hall light, and was greeted by the most horrific sight I had ever seen. I saw my father, on top of my mother, punching her in the face with all his might. That was the sound I heard; his fist hitting her face. I screamed for him to stop! He hit her a few more times. Then slowly stood up. I ran to help her. She was badly bruised, but quickly found her feet. He shouted obscenities at her! I screamed "Why?" He turned and looked at me with unapologetic eyes, picked up the nearby phone, and threw it at us. We ducked as it struck the refrigerator.

I stood there, shaking and confused. Who was this man? I didn't recognize him! I thought I knew him. I was daddy's little girl. We looked alike. We had the same dark, smooth skin that extended to our brown nail beds and blended seamlessly with our fingers. I inherited my singing voice from him. I thought he loved us! My father stripped my mom of her dignity, confidence, and beauty. The man who represented security for our family had become the violent intruder.

The beautiful, self-assured woman I had seen hours before was now disfigured and shaking from fear. The brief moment of certainty I felt earlier was stolen from me in a matter of minutes. Until that night, I'd never witnessed physical abuse; only heard the verbal confrontations.

I was 9 years old!

I had just been told that I needed a white or "high-yella" husband to ensure opportunities for my children. Now this? I was hopeless. My self-worth plummeted. I didn't know how to console my mom. I sat on the couch and cried with her. She held me and whispered, "Everything will be alright."

I was miserable. The bright future I envisioned for myself was now bleak. I wanted to yell, kick, scream, or anything to get rid of the pain! I needed to talk to anyone who would listen. Who could I trust? I knew I couldn't talk to anyone outside of our house because it was our business. My mom would say, "What happens in our house, stays in our house."

I learned how to mask my feelings--how to cry in the dark and smile in the light. I was proficient at telling people what they wanted to hear because no one really wanted to know the truth.

The image I had of my father shattered into a million pieces. I found out that his violent behavior had been the norm before I was born, and to add insult to injury, he was having relations with a light-skinned, long-haired woman. Wow! Talk about a blow to the face. I didn't know how to process any of this information. I was already dealing with the hurt caused by my grandmother's words, followed by the brutality I witnessed against my mother (by the very one who should have protected her), to now find out that my dad preferred light-skinned women. My small world imploded!

I was nine years old!

My innocent, young life had been turned upside down by two of the most influential people in my life. What was I going to do now? Who could I talk to about my feelings?

Truth is, I didn't know what I was feeling. I couldn't find the words to articulate what those moments had done to me. I cried every day. There was only one person that could make me feel better about myself, but he was 350 miles away.

Chapter Twelve

Secret from the Bayou

When I was little, my brother was my best friend. I followed him everywhere. The funny thing is, he let me. Our 10 year age difference didn't really seem to matter. We were always together. He even took me with him on a few dates. If I didn't like the girl...well, let's just say she didn't come around anymore. He was so cool! I think he liked being around me just as much as I liked being around him. No, I probably liked it more!

I remember this one time we were home alone, and I was sitting on the couch watching TV. I thought he was in his room, when all of a sudden the lights went out! I heard a familiar tune playing. It echoed down the hall. I was freaking out! I called out to my brother, "Where are you?"

"I'm right here. What's wrong?" he shouted.

Scared and confused, I nervously asked, "Why are the lights out? Are you playing that music?"

"I'll take care of it. I'm coming!" he said.

The music grew louder as a tall image began to walk toward me out of darkness! It looked like my brother, so I called out to him again. No answer this time! The silhouette got closer and I saw extended arms, reaching toward me. I screamed! Without warning, the lights flickered on and my brother appeared wearing a red and black leather jacket, dancing to Michael Jackson's "Thriller". Needless to say, he was successful in scaring the crap out of me. I still don't know how he did that! We had so much fun together. I missed him so much while he was away at college! He would always tell me how pretty I was, and that I could be and do anything I imagined. I believed him.

One weekend, my brother came home to visit from college. He brought a guest. She was a very beautiful girl. Upon first glance, she looked white, but she spoke with an accent so that dispelled the white theory. She wasn't black, at least I didn't think so. I thought she was just a friend from college. I later discovered that she was the woman he wanted to marry. I was angry! I didn't want to talk to her! I didn't want to know her! Not only had she successfully taken my best friend from me, the one who claimed to love me and my dark skin, she took my last bit of hope. I was counting on him to make me feel better about myself. He was the only one left to rescue me from the despair I felt. I was crushed. He was just like the others. My level of self-hate escalated to another level.

She had dark, long, bouncy hair. Sure she was nice and tried desperately to bond with me, but I hated her. She didn't know my secret. She didn't know what I'd been pondering over for the past few months. She was oblivious to the fact that she had just walked into the war that I was fighting and became the new enemy! She didn't know that I wanted to look like her. She didn't realize that the person who would always say I can be and do anything, wanted to marry the total opposite of what I thought he loved most about me.

What was I to do? Should I tell them my reasons for being so cold and distant? I had been ruined by those words that continued to echo in my ears... essentially telling me that I'm not good enough because I'm not light-skinned. I'm almost positive that I wouldn't have had the same response had they shown up a few months earlier, but the damage was done. My perception was my reality and everything that I would encounter moving forward, would be tainted by that implanted perception.

Chapter Thirteen

From Pain to Anger

My interactions with my grandmother became more and more infrequent. The times we did see each other, the atmosphere was cold and harsh. I didn't adore her anymore, so there was no reason to be nice. At times, I was totally disrespectful. Consequently, I received two unforgettable whippings in response to my lack of respect. The image is so vivid; the memory still fresh.

My mom and I stopped by Big Honey's house after a trip to town. I didn't want to chance sitting in her house with nothing for my hands to do, so I took a bag of candy and a book to keep me busy. I sat down on the floor, opened my candy and book, and pretended to be totally removed from the normal discourse: "How are you?" What brings you over here today?" Etc. Etc.

Soon, the questions began to float my way. I ignored them at first, faking my commitment to the book I deliberately brought. After mom called my name, I had no other choice than to hear what was being said. So, answering as if I had been shaken from a deep sleep, I said, "Huh? I'm sorry! Did you say something?"

Annoyed by now, my grandmother did something she despised. She repeated herself, "What did you buy from the store?" she said with clinched lips.

The words rolled off my tongue as though I'd rehearsed them, "What I wanted to get!" I said defiantly. Without warning, my mother leaped from her seat, with eyes fastened on me, and commenced to hitting any part of my body that wasn't shielded from the previous whack. Mom was upset and embarrassed, but most of all, disappointed. Was I wrong? Yes! I could have avoided that beat down. I was just so angry! I apologized, but it wasn't genuine. A part of me felt as though she knew I no longer wanted to be around her.

The next whipping would come by the hands of an unlikely candidate, my aunt. Our relationship was questionable at times. I couldn't tell if she liked me or hated me, but we managed to have a few good moments.

This particular day, my mom dropped me off to run errands for grandma, again! My aunt stopped by to visit. As usual, I was watching TV; being a good little girl. All of a sudden, I hear "Get up and empty that pot outside!" I looked up because I knew that command was directed at me. Everything was fine until that moment.

"*You* empty the pot outside." I protested.

My aunt proceeded to get a switch and whip me. I grabbed the pot I was instructed to empty and I started hitting her legs with it. Of course, she had the greater impact, but I tagged her a couple of times. Was I wrong? Yes! I should still be on the floor somewhere for that display of utter disrespect! I couldn't understand why this was happening! She had barely spoken to me that day. Then, out of nowhere, orders were being barked at me! I was mad!

Needless to say, our relationship was never really recovered. I thought I was going to get another whipping from my mom but surprisingly, she simply said, "You know better than that."

I did know better. I was sincerely sorry this time. No matter what I thought my aunt's intentions were at that moment, they in no way warranted that type of response from me.

However, I was ten. I didn't know how to verbally communicate my feelings. Yet, I needed to find a better way to deal with my anger. I had no one to talk to. I was alone.

Chapter Fourteen

Rude Awakening

The next few years were interesting. I was finally attending school in my hometown. I was about to be in middle school. Filled with anticipation of what the new school year would bring, yet fearful at the same time. I was entering a new territory. I was afraid of what my new peers would think of me. I was used to the ones from 5th grade, but middle school was a big deal. The summer leading up to middle school, I prepared to put my best face forward. I stayed out of the sun as much as possible. If I had to go outside, it was only for brief moments. My mother figured I was finally listening to her, and doing everything I could to prevent my complexion from darkening. She bought me fade cream and skin lightening soap. My daily routine consisted of cleansing, exfoliating, and moisturizing with products that guaranteed a lighter, brighter glow in a few short weeks. The packaging even had a model with a before and after picture. She was at least two shades lighter. I figured, if I followed the directions, and used it twice a day, I could achieve the same results. The more I used the soap and fade cream, the deeper I fell into my own delusion. I would look in the mirror and actually say, "I think it's working! My skin looks lighter!" I would finally be seen for the girl I felt I was on the inside- beautiful.

Well, school started, and it only took a day for the world I created to come crashing down. I was sitting in homeroom, and the teacher walked out to speak with another teacher. A boy sitting next to me, decides to ask me in front of a full, quiet classroom, "Why are you so black?" Shock and embarrassment quickly turned to anger and disgust! I replied sharply, "*You're* black too!" Then he proceeded to give me a lesson on the levels of blackness:

"No, I'm not black, I'm caramel! The girl in front of you is butterscotch, the boy behind you is a bit lighter than you, so we consider him milk chocolate. You're just black!"

I was horrified! This new classmate that I would have to sit next to for the entire school year, had just destroyed the little confidence I'd worked so hard to build over the summer, in a matter of minutes! I wasn't even good enough to be in a candy category like fudge or dark chocolate. I was just black! I was teased for weeks behind that one comment.

I think I was more upset with myself. I actually thought life would be different for me. My grandmother was right! I didn't have a chance in this world. No matter what I did to fit in, I would always be seen with "blacky-vision" glasses!

Luckily, I made a few good friends who didn't care about my complexion. They just liked being around me. I wouldn't have made it through sixth and seventh grade without them.

Chapter Fifteen

Anger Management

I fought a lot. I was suspended twice from school in sixth grade. I tried so hard to find other positive outlets, but nothing really helped. I calmed down a little at the beginning of seventh grade, but soon found myself in yet another fight. This particular fight was over a boy. I had never fought over a boy before, and I wasn't about to until she looked at me and said "You're too black for him anyway!"

In retrospect, I should have laughed considering this girl was just as dark, if not darker than I, and she was beautifully challenged. Laughable, right? I didn't laugh. I looked at the gathering crowd of pre-teen boys and girls provoking one of us to make a move. I wanted to walk away, but I couldn't. I charged at her full speed. I remember pushing her into the side of a bus. We were going blow for blow. Finally, one of my male classmates broke up the fight.

Afterward, all I could think of was how mad my mom would be… The last time I was suspended, she threw a chair at me, and almost hit my head. I'd never seen her so upset with me. I promised not to fight again. Well I broke that promise. I knew I would be suspended, especially since we were at another school working with the Special Olympics. Surprisingly, I wasn't suspended. I was so relieved!

I didn't want to fight anymore. I needed to change. I decided I was worth more than what I was I portraying.

Chapter Sixteen

Finding My Place

By eighth grade, I joined the school choir. I loved singing. I loved music even more. I spent most of my nights watching Video Soul and recording my favorite songs on cassette tape. I knew every R&B hit made from 1989-1992. I played the piano as well. So, I would listen to my cassettes and find the key of a song to play.

Music was my refuge. I sang any and everywhere; nursing homes, coronations, and school assemblies. I welcomed the new attention. No one cared about how I looked. They only wanted to hear the song of the week. My mom worked on talent show entries and showcases. I even won a few! I had a big voice and wasn't afraid to use it. My certitude in my talent, was undeniable. I didn't feel inadequate. I had something now that no one could take away from me; my voice!

I think my "aha" moment came during the coronation of my cousin who was voted queen of our high school in 1992. She was dark and lovely, like me, yet managed to win the votes of her peers. There was hope for me yet.

I was asked to sing "You bring me joy" by Anita Baker! Yay!!! My favorite artist! I practiced and practiced. Finally, the night had come to perform. I wore a gold gown adorned with sequins. I was so nervous. The gym was filled with classmates, parents, and teachers; my largest audience to date. The music started and I sang with all my might. During the climax of the song, the crowd erupted with applause, screams, and whistles! I was so proud of myself. I was fourteen, and the negativity and self-doubt I'd experienced up until that moment, paled in comparison!

I was afforded a great opportunity to meet a few people who were in the audience that night: a former member of a famous hometown band, and a male group that was preparing to record an album. I was asked to do a few background vocals and record a demo for a song written by one of the guys in the group. I was so excited!

I could finally see the light at the end of a very dark tunnel. I was free from this stigma! I was going to make something of myself, regardless of my skin color. But my mind had merely hidden those thoughts, while my heart cried out for more. My heart's cry would soon be answered.

I formed many friendships while working on the demo. One, in particular, grew into something for which I was not ready.

Chapter Seventeen

Hungry for Validation

One Tuesday, I was at the studio with the songwriter finishing the demo. I had a crush on him. He was older, talented...he looked at me and said, "You're so pretty"! He leaned in and kissed me. My heart stop beating. Everything was in slow motion. His words quieted my heart's cry and his touch awakened a part of me that I didn't know existed. I gave him a part of me that day that I would never get back. He was twenty-four, and I was still fourteen. He didn't know I was so young. I never told him my age. I was fully mature. He thought I was a senior and I never told him different.

He gave me something that the other men I loved, my father and brother, negated in their apparent betrayal to me: Validation! This guy didn't contradict his words with his actions. He knew what he wanted and he gave me what I needed. Unfortunately for me, validation came at a high cost. I allowed my heart to deceive me. I felt as though I'd died!

The next day, I was scheduled to sing at a banquet for the mayor. I sang "If I Could" by Regina Belle. It was a great night! Until I got home. Shortly after arriving, the phone rang. It was one of my good friends. She was hysterical! Crying uncontrollably, searching for the words to tell me…our third musketeer was killed that day! I couldn't breathe! I didn't hear what she said! I couldn't have! Did she say our friend was killed? She was fourteen! Who gets murdered at fourteen? She was shot! I was in disbelief.

The next day at school, all of her friends were in the cafeteria crying, but I didn't believe it. I wouldn't believe it. I thought it was a big joke, and she would eventually call me and say, "I'm fine Rhonda."

A funeral was scheduled for the upcoming Saturday; three days after the news of her death. She was very petite. The damage caused by the bullet, was so extensive that her body decayed at a rapid rate. I didn't want to go the funeral. I held on to the hope that no one would be at the church because she wasn't really dead.

I was sick at the sight of all of the cars. One in particular, the hearse. I walked in the church, and all I could do was stand there. I saw her laying in the casket. Grief consumed me. My knees buckled. My godmother was there to catch me. My heart ached! This was too much to bear! Two deaths in one week; one figuratively, and the other literally. My friend was gone! She was the one in whom I confided. She would have been the first to know about my life changing experience…but I was a day too late! I didn't have her to talk anymore.

Chapter Eighteen

Withdrawn

Changed forever, I decided to put my efforts and energy towards music. I was singing at least twice a week; not to mention the engagements scheduled by my school choir. I stayed busy to forget my pain. I hid in my music so I didn't have to deal with my shame!

I was alone. No one would understand what I was dealing with, so I kept quiet. I internalized every emotion. Maybe I was too afraid of what would come out of my mouth.

Would I ever be able to release all of this hurt?

Years would pass before I received the answer.

Chapter Nineteen

My Kin

In the midst of my chaotic life, I became an auntie to two beautiful girls. My sister was the first to give birth. Six months later, my brother's wife. Both were very fair-skinned. I didn't have any negative feelings toward them. They were innocent babies who just happened to inherit great genes.

I spent a lot of time with my oldest niece. She lived in close proximity to us. We visited my brother's new family often though. It was great going down to the "Big Easy"! So much to do; So many diverse people to see. I breathed in the culture as if it were my own. Being there helped me escape the monotonous routine of my life. I was free to dream without restrictions.

I had gotten past my hatred for my sister-in-law. I was older now and she was really sweet to me. I grew to love her.

During one of those visits, I overheard my brother's daughter ask her mom, "Why is my hair different from yours?" I can't remember her exact reply. In essence, she told her daughter it was due to resembling her father's side of the family more. My niece didn't like that answer. She wanted to look exactly like her mom. She had the right complexion, but she craved long, wavy, bouncy hair as well. I couldn't blame her. I did too! Life would be much easier for me! I wouldn't have to struggle anymore with the desire to be something I would never be...light-skinned.

I despised my thoughts. Maybe I was making a big deal out of nothing. Perhaps, I should just get over the cruel words spoken, and the selfish actions demonstrated and move forward.

That's what I would do. I'd move forward!

Chapter Twenty

Spirit Fingers

Sophomore year of high school…I remember it like it was yesterday. New challenges to meet; new faces to greet. I decided to venture outside of my comfort zone, way out of my comfort zone. I tried out for the varsity cheerleading squad. I must have been out of my mind. You see, not only was I dark-skinned, I was voluptuous too!

Cheer camp wasn't easy. I had the voice for it though. I even had the stamina. I couldn't jump like the rest of the squad, but I was strong and could support any stunt like nobody's business. Tryout day... I strutted on to the gym floor beaming with confidence. I nailed the routine. My jumps were still less than average, but my spirit was infectious! I made the squad! I think I was more proud of myself at that moment than when I received the standing "O" the previous year at the coronation. I was most proud because I didn't let my personal struggle hold me back. I knew what I wanted and I went after it. Singing was natural, but cheering required serious focus. It was hard work, and I loved it! I was thrilled to wear my purple and gold uniform. I can honestly say that for the first time, I felt feminine. A true girly-girl!

Chapter Twenty-One

She's Your Queen to Be

My newly discovered femininity peaked my interest in beauty pageants. My first pageant was more of an introduction to society. It wasn't based on beauty.

I was a debutante. I met girls from other schools and formed new relationships. We all looked and felt like princesses. We were elegant in our white gowns, as we promenaded across the event center floor to meet our lady-in-waiting. My father escorted me that night. It had been a long time since he made me smile, but he did that night!

By the time junior year started, I set my sights on a bigger crown. I wanted to be queen of my high school. I had to campaign, make a speech, and show off my talent! I had my circle of friends, but their votes alone wouldn't be enough to win. I had to meet and talk to as many schoolmates as possible. It was a lot of pressure!

Well, as luck would have it, I developed a bad case of Varicella; more commonly known as chicken pox. I was sixteen with chicken pox! I was covered with itchy, red blisters. I couldn't come out of the house, let alone campaign for queen. I still wanted to participate. So, I was given the option to record my speech along with a song of me singing to be played during the school assembly. My mother had my picture blown up and placed on the stage during the presentation. It was sad. Many of the underclassmen thought I had died. Subsequently, I lost.

I was depressed over it. I actually had another parent tell me that it was better this way and I shouldn't worry about being a queen. I should just keep singing because that was my true talent!

I was baffled! What did she mean? Was I only good for singing?

Her words struck a nerve in me. I stepped back and looked at the new queen and her court. It hit me like a ton of bricks. They were all light-skinned! I hadn't even thought about it like that! Was she implying that I never had a chance because I was dark-skinned? I thought, perhaps, I didn't win because I was sick and couldn't devote any time to the campaign. Whatever the reason, I was compelled to examine the situation more closely.

These girls were popular…but why? Were they popular because they represented the standard of beauty in our society? Or were they just friendly? I was friends with all of them; at least I thought we were friends. Nevertheless, the questions needed to be asked.

I talked to my grandmother about how I was feeling, and she emphatically stated, "The lighter you are, the righter you are."

Well, I had my answer. I should have never mentioned anything to her. I allowed her to speak yet another thing that perpetuated self-doubt. I was a fool to think that she'd have anything nice to say; even after watching me accomplish a few things over the past seven years.

I blamed myself.

Chapter Twenty-two

I'll Show You

Determined to prove that I was more than just a songbird, I decided to compete in a local competition that would showcase fitness, congeniality, speaking ability, and talent. There would also be objective judges to cast votes based solely on those four areas.

The competition was fierce. Girls from around the county came to compete and they all had a chance of winning. I needed to win. My ability to live my life, depended on it. There was so much riding on being the last girl standing.

After much preparation, the night to prove the naysayers wrong, had finally come. I was so nervous, but my desire surpassed my fear. I did everything in my power to stand out among the rest. I was ready to hear my name called.

The moment arrived to hear the results. My cheeks were shaking from smiling so much. My palms began to sweat as I stood there in anticipation.

I breathed a sigh of relief as the third runner up's name was called. It wasn't me. I had a chance.

"I think I won", I whispered to myself. The second runner up was called. Not me again! "Could this really happen for me?" I eagerly questioned. But before the excitement took root, I heard the MC say, "First runner-up goes to"…

"Did I hear my name?"

Yes, I did!

I thought for sure I had won the whole thing. I graciously walked to the space designated for the one who would stand proxy in the event the winner could not compete on the next level. I was devastated! I stood there smiling, doing everything I could to hold back the tears that wanted to flood my face.

I was happy for the winner though. She was a friend of mine. She was great in her own right, but I couldn't help noticing her very light skin. It was happening, yet again---those feelings of inadequacies. My talent, beauty, poise, and articulate speech were no match for the one who possessed all the same qualities, yet had one feature that would put her on top every time...her buttery hue. I was hurt. I knew that even if I was better than the best, I would only be called to stand in the 1st runner's up place. Could this really be my destiny?

As I supported my friend at the state competition, the answer to that question said a resounding yes. During the opening performance, I couldn't find her in the sea of vanilla. I didn't recognize her until she was right in front of our section. I was mad; not at her, but of what I knew, beyond a shadow of doubt, to be true. Lighter skin would always be the preference in this society.

What could I do now? I couldn't change my skin. I didn't know of a skin cream strong enough, at least not one that my mom could afford. I was sad for weeks. I thought about killing myself several times, but something wouldn't let me. I thought a lot about what I wanted to accomplish and how I would possibly be overlooked again and again because of my looks. I hated thinking that my life would be lived out in front of the disapproving eyes of critics. Never good enough, never pretty enough. Just cute, with stipulations. Why did I have to be pretty for a dark-skinned girl? Is that an accomplishment?

I was sick of life. I didn't belong here. I was sixteen going on seventeen and prepared to throw in the towel. I should have been thinking about senior prom, or college visits, or cheerleading...anything other than ending my life due to something that I had no control over.

I envied light-skinned girls. I thought they had it made. I believed every dark-skinned girl wanted to be the light-skinned girl who every boy wanted to date and every man wanted to marry. Wasn't that the trend? Small town high school football star turned pro athlete returns home with a mixed, Latin, or white chick...the trophy piece.

It wasn't entirely their fault. I believe that those boys/men saw the struggle of their dark-skinned mother or sister, and didn't want their future children to suffer the same plight.

It could be, they bought into the images portrayed by every media outlet and saw dark-skin as substandard and light-skin as the epitome of beauty.

Realizing that I would never know what it was like to be on the receiving end of such admiration is unnerving. I would inevitably be the admirer.

Chapter Twenty-Three

Big Fish

Eight years of an internal battle that started with a small seed had blossomed into a tree flourishing with self-doubt! I was lost, and living a double life. Full of confidence in front of my peers, but behind closed doors, tormented by the person I wanted to be; who I wished everyone saw. My love-hate relationship with my skin had turned into utter disgust. I wanted to peel it off. Why was every part of me so dark?

Was this really my lot in life? If so, I was ready to sell it to the highest bidder. Heck, I would have given it away…anything to be rid of this perpetual nightmare! I needed an alternative. I needed to see something different; do something different. Maybe, if I experienced something new, I could get over the pain of my past.

The questioned remained, "what to do now?" I knew I didn't want to stay on this emotional rollercoaster.

So, I decided to plan my next steps. First of which included finding a college far enough from home to start over, but close enough for mom to visit. This would be an easy task. I had a few scholarship offers; even from the local university, but I'd decided long ago not to attend that school. It wasn't a bad school. It was awesome. Unfortunately, it was five minutes from my house.

My sister told me of the time our mom showed up to her 8:00 class, and she was not there. Well, let's just say, there was hell to pay. I did not want to risk the chance of my mother showing up to a class that I would probably miss occasionally. So, staying at home was not an option. However, there was one school, far enough from home, that offered me free money to do what I love---sing.

When I was weighing my options between the liberal arts college that promised me a full ride, or the university that only offered the basics, I asked my high school choir director of which should I choose.

She playfully asked, "Do you want to be a little fish in a big pond, or a big fish in a little pond?"

I knew right away I wanted to be the big fish in a little pond. I wanted to go where everybody would eventually know my name. I was used to that. So big fish/little pond, is what I chose.

I was excited! I accepted the school's offer and looked forward to moving. For the first time in my life, I felt like things were working out for me. I was singing, cheerleading, and dating... (I literally just laughed out loud.)

Despite the many challenges, senior year was fun!

Chapter Twenty-Four

Courage to Move

For so long I'd played it safe; doing the right things so people would like me. I had been living my life for others. Now, it was time to live for me, to have new experiences, and discover who I was underneath all the layers of deceit. I had the opportunity to reinvent myself.

I would be leaving for school soon, but making the transition would prove to be emotionally draining. The violence in my home, though few and far between, was still happening. I didn't want to leave my mom behind, yet I couldn't stay and forfeit this chance at a new life.

I was terrified.

My mom and I spent a few days talking and reminiscing about our lives and our expectations for the future. I knew she was heartbroken about my soon departure, but her sadness grew as we cleaned out my closet.

Underneath the pile of stuffed animals, board games, and clothes rested a letter. It was written on the wide-lined, brown paper for beginning writers. I must have written it in preschool or kindergarten. In the letter, I begged her to take us away from here. "Less leeve" I shakily wrote.

Though misspelled, the words leaped off the page and chilled the room. The handwriting was wobbly. I must have been scared at that moment; probably from an argument I'd overheard. I was easily frightened by the sound of my father's voice. It rumbled like the thunder.

Finding that letter made us realize that we were far from healed. We cried that night.

Chapter Twenty-Five

My New Home

It was quiet during the two hour drive to my new home. A familiar silence---the kind I experienced when we took my brother to college ten years prior. Once we arrived in the new city, we went to the store. My mom bought everything I needed to fill my dorm room: bedding, trash can, refrigerator, toiletries, shower shoes, and groceries... Just to name a few.

I remember the relief I felt as we pulled up on campus for the first time. The air was different. I could breathe easier. This would be my home for the next four years. It took us a little more than an hour to unload, clean, and organize my side of the room. It was quick and easy. I was settled in my new room.

We walked around campus and met some interesting people. Another hour or so had passed before I told mom that I would be ok, and she could leave if she was ready.

Though she wasn't, the woman that I'd grown to admire for her tenacious spirit, conceded to my request. We hugged. A few seconds felt like an eternity in her arms. I was sure to long for those comforting arms in the near future. However, I had to let her go so I could embark on my journey. She smiled with her lips, but couldn't hide the sadness in her eyes.

Through streaming tears, I watched as she slowly drove away.

Chapter Twenty-Six

The "Crab" Year

Freedom! I didn't know what to do first! Operation, "reinvent me" was in full effect.

I walked into the student center and started introducing myself to everybody. I wanted everyone to know my name. "Where did this girl come from?" I asked myself. I even had a new walk. I was ready! I wore confidence like a new pair of shoes…uncomfortable at first, but after they're broken in, the perfect fit! I liked who I was becoming.

Singing with my choir mates gave me the best moments from that year---perfecting my craft with some of the most talented people on this side of the Mississippi River. It was amazing! I didn't have one encounter with a person questioning my complexion. No one made me feel inadequate.

In fact, more people told me how flawless my skin appeared and how pretty I was than ever before. I couldn't have asked for more. However, that's what I got.

Chapter Twenty-Seven

Him

One day, early fall of 1996, I walked downstairs to the lobby of my residence hall, and saw him sitting there with 2 of his friends. He spoke. I spoke. Some way or another, we found a way to keep talking.

He was different from any guy that I'd liked in the past. The major difference---our beliefs. I was hesitant because of that, but I was open. This was the new me; prepared for an adventure. I didn't want a relationship; just a friend. Mainly because I decided a long time ago not to fall in love. Love was messy and hurtful. No! Fun was all I intended to have. To my amazement, it soon blossomed into something more.

By spring, we were inseparable. I was pleasantly surprised by him. He made me happy. I allowed myself to be vulnerable around him. I wasn't restricted or afraid to try new things with him. I was comfortable in my skin. Before him, I'd mastered the ability to stay unattached, especially with matters of the heart. But there I was, falling…

He complimented daily. He thought I was beautiful. Unbeknownst to him, he was feeding the part of me that had been malnourished for so long. Though I knew our relationship was more than just him fulfilling that part of me, I also knew that we wouldn't have lasted had he not. Every previous relationship, I had to have control. I didn't want to get hurt, even though I hurt others. He made me put my guard down…though only for a moment.

Chapter Twenty-Eight

Turn for the Worse

The end of that year brought about new and exciting firsts in my life. New friends…new love. After school dismissed, I went home for a few weeks to pick up my car. Yes! I'd be taking my car back to college! No more walking to the grocery store for my Ramen noodles and peach soda! I could drive!

The few weeks I spent at home went by without incident. It was peaceful. I returned to school to attend a summer session and get a jump start on sophomore year. Summer school was fun, but it went by in a flash. Before I knew it, regular classes were in session.

Shortly after fall classes resumed, my car started acting up. I didn't know what was wrong. So, I called the only person that could fix it, or at least pay to get it fixed---my father. I asked him to come and check it out. I was actually excited to see him…especially since we had a good time earlier in the summer.

That changed when he pulled up though.

He called to let me know that he was in the parking lot. He had a spare key, so by the time I walked downstairs, he was already under my hood looking for the problem.

We hugged and I thanked him for coming. A few minutes passed before I noticed his truck. It was conveniently parked several spaces from my car. I saw someone sitting in the passenger seat. My body went numb. The excitement of seeing him swiftly turned into regret. I stared at him. He finally acknowledged my glare and smirked like only he could.

"What's wrong?" he knowingly inquired.

In the most sarcastic, and disrespectful voice I could muster up I said, "I should ask you that!"

He had a puzzled look on his face.

"Why are you confused?" I demanded. "You just drove 165 miles down here with another woman, and you thought I would be ok with that?"

He shrugged me off. I walked away. I had every intention of going back to my room, but I found myself walking toward his truck; then standing behind his truck. Finally, face to face with this woman who I'd never seen before. I thought I was having an out of body experience or something because I heard myself say,

"Hi! Who the hell are you?"

She gasped in disbelief and whispered, "I'm your dad's friend."

"My father doesn't have friends who are women, so what kind of friend could you possibly be?" I snarled.

"Just a friend," she protested.

"You know he's married?" I snapped.

She emphatically said, "Yes!"

By this time, my dad had joined us. By the look on his face, I knew he was aggravated by my interrogation. He was angry! I didn't care! It was apparent that he didn't care either; about me or my mother.

In an instant, all of the work I'd put into rewiring my thinking, was proven pointless. He broke me! Again! Not just by bringing another woman, but by flaunting his preference. She was plain, but she was light-skinned with long hair.

Memories of my childhood flooded my mind. Feelings of inadequacy overtook me. He awakened the sleeping giant that had tormented me most of life…the thing that I thought was gone.

I was nine all over again. The scab was ripped off! As I stood there emotionally bleeding, I watched this man, my father, get into his truck and drive away. He didn't even fix my car!

I ran to the bathroom and looked in the mirror hoping to see the girl that I was fighting so hard to become, only to be repulsed by the sight of the girl I never escaped…reminding me that I would never be good enough!

I threw up!

Chapter Twenty-Nine

The Morning After

I awakened with hopes that it was all a dream. But as I motioned closer to the mirror, I saw my puffy red eyes. I'd cried myself to sleep and probably cried while I slept. I wanted to call my mom and tell her what happened. I should've called her the same day, but I couldn't. I was worried for her.

My dad always took his anger out on her, even though nine times out of ten, she was not the cause. I finally called her just to make sure she was alright. I couldn't tell if anything had happened. She sounded happy. Maybe she was just happy to hear from me. Nonetheless, her voice didn't betray her. She was skilled in the art of concealing her true feelings. There was no need in disrupting what sounded to be a pleasant day for her, so I didn't tell her about dad's shenanigans. I talked as if nothing

Momma, I Wanna be Light-skinned

had happened…but something did happen. I was forced to remember the moment I met self-doubt; when she disproved everything I thought I knew about myself.

Seeing my father sport his trophy piece so boldly in front of me, his daughter, the daughter he endearingly referred to as "Cookie", made me revert to that little girl that told him I'd never get married because of him. The woman that I was becoming, or better yet wanted to be, was long gone.

I turned inward to the familiar place that had protected my heart. That place that I alone had access. It was lonely, but it was safe.

My safe place.

108 | P a g e

Chapter Thirty

Whenever, Wherever, Whatever

My guard was back up. The one that I'd let in for that brief moment had been kicked out. He didn't know it. I, like my mom, knew how to conceal my feelings. I loved him, yes! But I was my daddy's child. I enjoyed a little variety. So, I went back to having fun with him and a few others! I didn't want to be this way, but I felt in control being this way, or so I thought. Perhaps, I was just afraid of more rejection.

The people who were supposed to love me more than any outsider, had shown me on more than one occasion that I was inadequate. So, how could anyone truly love me? I searched for someone to fix my brokenness; someone to tell me that I was enough; someone to see the beauty within me without criticizing my external.

No amount of intimate encounters I had could fill the emptiness that I felt---and believe me, I tried. But the more I tried, the more I saw pieces of me scatter. The hollow corridors of my heart echoed my thoughts...a rhythmic beating of despair and desperation. Was there no end to this torment?

I felt ashamed. There was no one to talk to. No one who could understand what it was like for me to wake up every morning, walk to the mirror, and hope that the image seen the night before, had somehow changed into the image I envisioned in my dreams.

I was embarrassed to be a nineteen year old sophomore in college, still functioning with a nine year old's heart...the disappointments, the hurt, and the confusion.

I needed another option. I needed to know that my life was worth more than the sum of my bad experiences.

Chapter Thirty-One

The Encounter

I remember giving my hand to my pastor and my heart to the Lord at a young age. I remember being baptized. I remember waking up every Sunday morning to the sound of gospel music blasting down the hall; to the smell of bacon and eggs for breakfast---baked chicken, greens, lima beans, and cornbread for dinner. My mom had it all done before 11:00 service. She was bad like that!

I remember listening to her pray to God, thanking Him for all that He had done and was going to do for our family. I even heard her praying for my father. Praying that he'd be forgiven; praying that God would heal him from his hurt…though he'd hurt her.

I remember seeing God answer her prayers. She often prayed that God would bless us financially. My mom was a teacher and was paid once a month, so there would often be more month left than money.

One time, in particular stands out. I'm sure it was near the end of the month, because we didn't have much money. We needed dinner, so we went to the grocery store. Before we got out of the car, mom said, "We can only get some pork-n-beans and weenies. So don't ask for anything else."

As we approached the store, she put her arm in front of me and said, "Wait!" I asked her what was wrong but she didn't answer. She just stared at the sidewalk. Finally, she spoke.

"Do you see that?" she asked.

"See what?" I questioned.

She bent over, and removed a neatly folded, hundred dollar bill from a crack in the sidewalk. It looked as if someone had just stuck it in there right before we got out of the car. I stood there in awe. God had done it again.

There were other times that I encountered God through my mom, but I'd yet to experience His power personally.

He was about to make Himself known to me.

Chapter Thirty-Two

The Encounter Part 2

On October 3, 1997, I was invited to church with a friend of mine. It was a Friday night. I'll never forget it. I experienced something so amazingly indescribable. I felt freedom like never before. I caught a glimpse of what my life was supposed to exemplify. I saw myself without restraints. I was confident, fearless, and complete. My life changed that night.

My current situation had yet to acknowledge the change, but I was different. I discovered another option. I no longer wanted to be the girl that needed to hear the approval of others to feel worth something. I didn't want to be the girl that found comfort in the arms of a man, and identity in his words. I owed it to myself to find out who God intended me to be. I owed it to the God of my mother to let Him be more than enough for me---to be my God.

It wouldn't be easy to change my perception. I'd been living in an alternate reality that was created for me, yet accepted and fostered by me. It was time to shed the fear, shatter the false image, and rise to meet the challenge of accepting me.

Chapter Thirty-Three

In the Meantime

I struggled with believing the newly heard Word and holding on to what held me for so long. It had taken years to frame my way of thinking. It would be too hard to change. The encounter with God showed me that I needed to renew my mind in order to change my thoughts. So even though I had this experience, I would still have to make a daily decision to accept change. Was I worth it? I didn't know. All I knew, was what I knew; not what I'd yet to experience.

I was torn. I felt as though I was the rope in the tug of war, pulled by two opinions. On one side was God telling me who I was supposed to be, and who I always was. Yet, on the other side, I heard the old voice telling me what I would never become.

I didn't know what to believe. Would I believe the one who whispered something so soothing, yet hard for me to comprehend? Or would I hold on to my security blanket? I knew what rejection and pain felt like. I was insulated by it...it protected me from the anticipation of acceptance.

Hearing I have value and purpose was a melody I'd heard before, but never in this key. It struck chords that I never knew existed on my piano of life. It made me hope. It made me dream. It became a symphony in my ear, and I wanted to listen to it over and over again.

Slowly, I began to shed the stinking thinking to which I had grown accustomed. I threw away my security blanket and embraced something new.

I was worth it. I was worth the fight.

Chapter Thirty-Four

I See the Light

The rest of that year had its expected ups and downs. I made it through without incident. Nineteen ninety-eight was a year of anticipation. One dream, which I'd dreamed of since a young girl, would finally be realized. However, it would not come without much preparation.

I remember the first time I heard the clarion call of these women. They were approaching the university's football stadium in my hometown. It was homecoming, many years ago. I was listening to the band, when all of a sudden, I heard an all-encompassing crescendo of a sustaining note. I was captivated. It permeated the arena. It was magnificent. I looked up to see a promenade of red walking down the hill. I asked the girl next to me, "who are they and what do I have to do to be a member?"

Now, eleven years later, the time of manifestation was drawing near.

I was a junior in college by now and I'd had a few years to build a great rapport with some of my future sisters. More than that…we were friends. The memory is still vivid- the butterflies in my stomach during my interview, to the overwhelming excitement of being chosen, and the lifelong bonds formed by the "31". Our probate show was one for the books. We arrived on campus in a motorcade filled with motorcycles and SUV's. We were fitted in our indigo, boot-cut jeans, white crisp shirts, and the all so lovely, khaki paraphernalia jackets sporting our line name and number. "100% Diva" was the name given to me. I was number 18. The show was flawless. I lived in that moment for weeks! I'd never been so proud of myself. The experience was life changing.

I learned a lot about myself during that process, but the real lesson was about to be learned.

Chapter Thirty-Five

The Awakening

After I lost my campaign for high school queen to my lighter-skinned opponents, I thought perhaps, I could be a college queen. I knew there would be challenges to overcome being the fluffy, dark-skinned girl that I was, but others who looked like me, had accomplished it. So, why not me?

With that very question in mind, I put my plan into action. I let others know of my future endeavor. I rallied the support of many. It was humbling. No one cared about my complexion or fluffiness. All they cared about was who I was as a person, and how I treated them.

Despite the internal chaos that was going on in my life, I still managed to love others. I was consistent with them, and my peers appreciated that.

However, the journey to the throne would not come without controversy. One of my beautiful, talented, and popular sisters also had the same goal in mind. I had no problem competing with her. However, other sisters thought it would cause the overall support of the student body to divide. Wanting to look like a united force, some of my sisters proposed that we present our platform to all the sisters…followed by a vote that would decide which of us would represent our sisterhood. The votes were tallied, and I'd been chosen by my sisters to represent our sisterhood in the upcoming campaign for campus queen.

I told my family. They immediately began strategizing for the weeks ahead. They purchased t-shirts, cups, and banners all saying, "Vote for Rhonda". It was happening so fast.

A few days later, I received a call about a new vote being conducted. The reasons disclosed should have been irrelevant since a majority vote was cast initially. I didn't like it, but I presented my platform anyway. Votes were tallied again, but this time I was out and she was in. I was shattered! I respectfully conceded in that moment. I don't know why, but I said ok.

I understood their change of heart though. All of the options had to be weighed: a fluffy, dark-skinned girl like me, competing against two physically fit, two shades lighter than me, though equally talented, girls like them…I was bound to lose. I went to my car and called my boyfriend. He rushed out of his dorm and I cried on his shoulder.

He simply asked me, "What do you want?"

"I want to run! I know I can win this!" I emphatically stated.

I was tired of taking a back seat to what others thought of me. I'd lived my life thinking that if I please this one and that one, then I'd be liked. If I just did what they asked and be the person they wanted me to be, then I would be enough- but I would never be enough for anybody until I started being enough for me.

Sitting in my car, with tears flowing down my face, I heard God say, "It's your time!"

I told my boyfriend, and he said, "Go back in there and tell them you're running anyway!" So I did!

I realized that none of my sisters knew what I was dealing with; I never shared my personal struggle. I don't believe anyone intentionally set out to hurt me. I'd shown my peers exactly what I wanted them to see. Everyone thought I was strong and confident, but up to this point, I was a scared little girl; desperately seeking approval and acceptance.

This was not about them. It was not about causing discord. It was all about me. For the second time in my life, I made a choice to choose me. It was the best decision I could have made.

I ran my campaign with diligence and class. I had the hardest working friends around me helping to get the message out. My face was all over the campus. It was the most exhilarating and nervous fun I'd ever had.

There was a pageant before the election. I sang "Still I Rise" by Yolanda Adams. My favorite line in that song says, "Yet still I rise! Never to give up; never to give in against all odds."

During a time when seemingly all odds were against me, those words confirmed my decision. The beauty of that moment rests in the fact that I chose that song before any of the aforementioned details occurred. How powerful was that? I'd come full circle. I was proud of myself! I didn't give up or give in to the pressure which wanted me to do just that.

I ultimately won. My peers chose me. I was honored. Finally, at age twenty, I could look in the mirror and see beauty. I no longer looked at myself through the eyes of my grandmother or childhood critics. I was free!

Months later, I graced the front page of my hometown newspaper, and joined other royals in Ebony magazine's HBCU Campus Queens edition. Oh, what a feeling! The culmination of years of living beneath who I could be, were over. I no longer looked in the mirror with disapproving eyes. I was finally free!

My eyes were open to the possibility that maybe all that I'd been told, and all that I'd experienced, were merely versions of someone else's truth for their life, that I'd just proven to be a lie for mine.

Chapter Thirty-Six

Left without Answers

Many transitions occurred over the next few years. I graduated from college, and began working toward building a life for myself. I underwent many losses during that time; friendships, relationships, but none as significant as the loss I was about to experience.

It was June of 2002. I went home to have my wisdom teeth removed. I was nervous. This would be my first time under anesthesia. I'll never forget the anxiety I felt as I walked through the doors of the oral surgeon's office. My dad was there. One of the rare and special moments I remember having with him. Seeing my fear, he put his hand on my shoulder and said, "It'll be over before you know it and I'll be here waiting for you."

He put my mind at ease, and sure enough, as quickly as I went in, I was leaving out. I felt like I'd taken a long nap. I was woozy though. My father was right there. He walked beside me as the nurse pushed me in the wheelchair towards the exit. I must have fallen asleep in the car because the next thing I remember was waking up in my bed. I suppose dad heard me stirring because he peeked his head in the door and asked if I was ok. I told him I was fine, but hungry. He made me some soup. My dad didn't cook, so seeing him go to the kitchen, open a can of chicken noodle soup, warm it in the microwave, and bring it to me, was definitely a treat. He seemed happy to do it. I remember him being attached to me that day. He was attentive and very talkative. He reminisced about his childhood and my childhood. He even told me how much he loved my mother. I didn't know it then, but I think in some way, dad was trying to make amends with me.

He sang to me. I went to sleep.

That was Monday.

The next morning I got up and got ready to return to my home. Dad had already gone to work. I called him to let him know that I was about to leave. He asked me to wait until he came home for lunch, so I did. He arrived around noon. I was all packed and ready to go. We sat and talked for about fifteen minutes. I knew I couldn't stay much longer because I had to take care of some things back home before the next day. He asked me to stay. I told him I had to go back to work. He asked again. I wanted to stay, but I had to get back. I hugged him and thanked him for taking care of me. He told me he loved me and I returned the same words. Then I left.

That was Tuesday.

The next day, I went to work thinking about my time at home. For the first time in years, I wanted to go back. So, I decided to make plans to return that weekend, but my plans would be altered.

I received a call from some of my friends asking me to meet them at church after I got off work. I thought it was an odd request, but I obliged. We met and they told me to get in the car and come with them to my house. I was nervous by now. I knew something was wrong. I asked them to tell me the problem and they insisted that everything was alright. I knew better. We arrived at my apartment and they told me to call home. I was scared, but I called anyway. My mom answered! I was relieved by the sound of her voice.

Through sobs, she told me that my dad had died. "He had a heart attack around noon", she said. Eerily close to the same time that I'd left the previous day.

My emotions were all over the place. I was mad at myself because he asked me to stay, but I didn't. I was heartbroken because I wouldn't have the chance to run back home, and tell him I love him, but relieved because he gave me such a sweet memory in the days prior. He'd shown me the type of father that he was capable of being.

Then, I got angry all over again because he had died and left me with so many questions. Questions that I thought only he could answer. Questions like, "Why did you wait until I was 22 to show me that I was worth your attention?"

"Why didn't you rescue me from my torment as a little girl?"

"Didn't you know that I hated myself and you were part of the reason?"

But it was too late. I was left with the memory of his potential. I had two choices: continue asking questions that he couldn't answer, or accept the peace in knowing that he spent the last two days of his life trying to make up for the past thirteen years of mine. I chose peace. I'm so thankful to God for allowing me to have those days with my father.

Chapter Thirty-Seven

Love the Hurt Away

Several months had passed since the death of my father. I was still grieving. Every day was an emotional rollercoaster. I chose peace but I wanted to give it back. I wasn't ready to release him. I didn't want to surrender the pain that I was so comfortable feeling.

I was just going through the motions. I wasn't as active in church. I wasn't smiling as much. Eventually, I withdrew from friends. I was in a low place. One night at church, my pastor told me it was time to snap out of it and let God heal me. His words were painful yet true. But I really didn't know how to let go of my pain. So, I did the only thing I could do…cry. I cried many nights over the past four months, but this time my tears seemed to yield a release. I felt months of pressure, anxiety, and anguish fall from me as I poured out my pain on my living room floor. I slowly returned to myself. I started laughing again. And as I continued to surrender my hurt, God continued to love it away.

Every passing day was better than the day before. I was being healed not only from the most recent events in my life, but from past hurts, disappointments, and mistakes. I felt as though the slate was clean, and I could start again.

Chapter Thirty-Eight

My Intended

In November of 2002, I started a new chapter in my life. I was finally honest with myself and a great friend of mine. I admitted to having more than just platonic feelings for him. In fact, those friendly feelings departed several years ago after we shared our first kiss. However, out of fear of losing a friend, we decided to abandon the thought of something more and preserve our friendship.

Our thoughts on the subject were different now. We were older and ready to explore the possibility of a new kind of love.

We took it slow at first, but fell madly in love over the next year. Christmas of 2003, he secretly expressed his intent to marry me to my mother and brother. I'm still shocked that neither of them said anything to me about it. However, Valentine's Day of 2004, my honey let me in on the secret. He didn't propose, but he told me he was making plans to secure a more permanent role for me in his life. I was expectant, yet tickled to hear him say it at the same time.

In July, on my birthday, he made good on his word. I knew we were going out to celebrate my birthday, but I had no idea of the surprise in store. He planned a party for me at a restaurant with several friends. Everyone was eating and having fun. Then, I noticed my friend walking toward the table with a cake. Everybody sang the birthday song as she approached and placed the cake in front of me. As I looked down to blow out the candles, I noticed a sparkle that wasn't from a candle. My love kneeled next to me and proposed in front of our friends. It was perfect! We were married on October 24th and by April 2005, we were pregnant.

Since getting married, I hadn't suffered many issues with confidence or lack thereof. I was loving me and loving my husband. Through our courtship, and our marriage, he had managed to love me to the point of amnesia. I'd forgotten what it was like to doubt myself. But now, facing the opportunity to bring life into this world, caused those old feelings and memories to resurface.

When I was younger, I used to say how I wanted to have 6 boys; my own basketball team with an alternate. Now, the time had come and I was petrified. It dawned on me that I could have a little dark-skinned girl. A girl that would undoubtedly look like me. I didn't want that. I didn't want her to go through what I went through. I didn't want the hard task of convincing her that she was beautiful, though others may not think the same. How could I teach her to love herself? I knew I couldn't! How could I teach what I'd yet to learn and accept for myself? For weeks, I pondered how having a little girl would affect me. With the news of a little boy coming, I didn't have to worry about it anymore. I knew my son would resemble his dad. At least, I hoped as much.

Delivery day was finally here! I was so eager to meet this little baby boy. But the excitement left my face when I saw him. He didn't resemble me at all. I didn't smile. I just stared in disbelief. The doctor didn't know how to respond. He finally stuttered, "Congratulations?" He made it sound like a question. My husband looked at me and was also stunned by my lack of enthusiasm. I was too busy looking at the light-skin on my new baby. He was everything I wanted…yet I still wasn't happy.

I pushed those feelings aside as I held him for the first time. He opened his eyes and looked at me. I fell in love. My momentary relapse was just that; momentary. I decided not to question, but to delight in this moment.

Chapter Thirty-Nine

Back Down Memory Lane

My first year as a mom was filled with restless nights and power nap days. I never knew that watching a baby sleep could be so fulfilling. He brought me so much joy. I thought I knew my capacity to love, but he stretched me even more. He found a place in my heart that I didn't even know was there.

All was going well, when tragedy struck again. My grandma died. I didn't know how to feel. I was sad because she was my grandmother, my mom's mom, and the matriarch of our family. She was the point of reference for our lineage and our identity. I was an extension of her.

On the other hand, I was upset because I would never have a chance to tell her how she made me feel on that pivotal night. I would never get to ask her why she said what she said. I would never know why she didn't offer me any other option besides marry a white of light-skinned guy. She would never know the power of her words. We had unfinished business. Her words marked the beginning of my journey. She acted as the writer in my life and told me my destination before I even began. My perception of the world and myself was forced on me by her. And now the answers to the uncertainty about my worth, would be buried with her.

Unlike my father, my grandmother and I didn't create any last minute, happy memories. I was left with memories of insufficient sentiments. So instead of confronting those feelings, I repressed them.

Several months later, my husband and I found out that we were expecting our second child. This pregnancy was different. I was sick most of the time. I was convinced that I was having a girl. Fear overtook me. I was petrified yet again at the thought having a little girl. I was pleased to know that I was having another boy. My mind was at ease.

I was embarrassed by my own thoughts. I didn't realize the depth of disdain I had for myself. I didn't want to believe that twenty-six words spoken so many years ago were now established. I had indeed married a light-skinned man and given birth to even lighter-skinned babies. My involuntary quest was now complete. I had all the necessary parts to ensure endless opportunities for my children. They were light, so I knew they would be alright!

Chapter Forty

The Hard Truth

One morning while in the shower, I was overcome with emotion. I began to cry. I heard my grandma's words ringing in my ear. I saw all of the circumstances that caused me to accept her words. The reality, is that I was thirty year's old, still seeing myself from a nine year old's perspective. I was subjugated by a moment. In spite of all that I'd accomplished, I still didn't feel good enough.

But I was tired of feeling this way. I was tired of being comfortable in my pain. I was ready to learn something new, but I couldn't release years of toxic thinking without having something else to replace it. I was determined to leave that familiar place of fear. I couldn't afford to live one more day in defeat!

Chapter Forty-One

The Process

I came to the realization that most of my past decisions were made from a broken place---a place of desperation and longing. I'd relinquished my power and embraced the opinions of others. So much so, that their thoughts became my reality. I didn't know how to make decisions that could possibly preserve me from self-destruction. The process has been long. I even tried to run from it a time or two. I knew that exposing and dealing with the innermost parts of my heart would cause me pain, and possibly discomfort for those closest to me. But writing has been my balm, and as a result, I no longer suffer in silence and in fear of someone saying, "That's not what really happened!" or "Get over it already!"

I tried to get over it. But I couldn't be free until I released everything and everyone that got me to this place. Including me! Only then would I regain the power over my own story. I didn't have a say in how my story began, but I can be confident of the greatness that will show forth in the end.

My path to wholeness is simple; not easy. I had to forgive, create a new mindscape, embrace my uniqueness, understand my worth, and make new connections. I endeavored to begin again by making decisions from a secure place; a complete place.

Chapter Forty-Two

Step by Step

"Life becomes easier when you learn to accept an apology you never got." ~ Robert Brault ~

Forgiveness is a powerful tool. If used, it can propel you to your next level. If ignored, it will most definitely stifle your progress. The secret? *You*. You have the power to choose to forgive, or not. Letting go can be the hardest thing to do. When you internalize negative words for so long, they appear as truth. Subsequently, your internal response causes you to accept, repeat, believe and ultimately embody someone else's perception. You must realize that forgiveness is never about the other person; it's about you. If they never apologize, you still have to move forward. The things that have happened to us are probably long forgotten by the other person. Whether it happened 5 months or 5 years ago, release them. It won't be easy, but you deserve to be free.

Forgiveness gives way to creating a new outlook. As I forgave others for the words spoken over me, and forgave myself for the words I accepted and spoke over my life, I learned how to exchange negative words for life giving declarations. I embraced new possibilities with my words.

For example, I swapped "You're so black" for "I have flawless skin!"

I traded "You're pretty to be so dark" for "I'm beautiful without contingency!"

I threw away the lie that said, "You won't have a chance in this world" and embraced the truth that declares, "I can accomplish anything I set my mind to do!"

Stop waiting on the right moment to change. Create change with your own words.

Until you create a new mindscape, you will
continue to deprive yourself of experiencing the
real you. Heretofore, you've displayed the replica
implemented by others, and embraced by you; with
hopes that you'd fit in or be accepted. It's time to
shed that inherited idea and be the original God
intended you to be. There is no one like you, on
purpose. There is a specific intention wrapped up
in your uniqueness. Embrace it! Every moment
you waste trying to be what you think others want
you to be, the world misses out on who they need
you to be.

Chapter Forty-Three

Press Delete

Stop rehearsing the pain of your past, by replaying the messages they left on the recorders of your heart. Your worth is not contingent upon others telling you who you are. It's not predicated upon relationship. You are worth it! Period! And when you know that, you'll attract the right relationships.

As a child, I couldn't decipher between what messages to delete or save. Everything needed to be stored. But as I matured, I realized that being in a relationship with someone, does not instinctively produce a healthy predisposition. In fact, it may have caused me to behave contrary to what I've always known. I deserved better than what I was offered, yet thirsting for approval, I accepted adverse comments as heartfelt admonition. Which is why the things I heard as a child, continued to echo in my ear as a teen, and ultimately became a voice of reasoning as an adult. I was comfortable with that voice. I was guided by it. But that comfort caused the dysfunction in my life.

I was consumed with rehearsing the reasons for my lack of progress in life, instead of discovering how I could change my trajectory. I know now, that my poor self-image was a learned behavior. Thankfully, I could learn all over again.

Chapter Forty-Four

Uniquely You

How do you heal? How do you forget? At what point in your life do you choose to let go and love yourself?

I know it may be hard for you to believe right now, but there will be a defining moment in your life when your opinion of yourself is all that matters. You are unique-- A one of a kind, special edition! No one else can beat you being you. Do you know how empowering that is? You are the first, the only, and the last of you! Your looks, personality, and experiences embody a specific task that can only be accomplished by you. So many people go through life thinking that God made a mistake when He created them. That's nonsense! He made you an original. Don't insult Him by being a carbon copy of someone else. You are a masterpiece.

Just think about all of the priceless and revered art. Some have odd angles and intricate patterns. Some are asymmetrical. Others are controversial in theme. What do they have in common? Most weren't appreciated for their unique beauty in the beginning. They were considered unusual; ugly even. But in the eyes of the one who created them, every angle was perfect. Every flaw was magnificent.

You too are wondrous! Extraordinary! Molded in the hands of a loving potter. No matter what you think your inadequacy may be, know that God has purposed you for greatness!

Chapter Forty-Five

My Resolve

If I have learned anything on this journey to self-acceptance, it's that I am more than my complexion. I am more that my mistakes, my disappointments, and my accomplishments. My thirty plus years of adventure culminate with the resolve…I just want to be me! The one who dreams of soaring high above the clouds like birds in the sky. The one who whispers sweetly to the wind in hopes that it will carry my song in its breeze. The "me" who stares adversity in the face and welcomes its challenge because I know it will take me to my destined place. And though this "me" is still becoming, I've embraced the "me" that is dark-chocolate, strong, courageous, confident, and full of faith. I've embraced that my road to acceptance was about me being a life saver for others. A buoy to those of you being tossed by the waves of self-doubt that's deterring you from making the decision to choose you. I serve as a marker to point you in the direction of decision.

Today is your day to decide that your future is worth the fight. Decide today to take this opportunity to share with the world the "you" that was created with purpose. You are enough! You have everything that you need to accomplish anything.

Decide today to be the best you forever.

Now that I've told you my story, I invite you to tell yours. Write as if no one else will read it. It's time to be uniquely you.

Momma, I Wanna be Light-skinned

Rhonda Bennett

Momma, I Wanna be Light-skinned

Rhonda Bennett

_____

_____

_____

_____

_____

_____

_____

_____

_____

_____

_____

_____

_____

_____

_____

_____

_____

_____

_____

Momma, I Wanna be Light-skinned

_____

_____

_____

_____

_____

_____

_____

_____

_____

_____

_____

_____

_____

_____

_____

_____

_____

_____

_____

_____

_____

About the Author

Rhonda Bennett is a native of Tuskegee, Alabama. She received a Bachelor of Arts degree in English from Stillman College in Tuscaloosa, AL, where she became a member of Delta Sigma Theta Sorority, Inc.

A mother of two extremely charismatic boys, Rhonda understands the importance of creating an environment that promotes success in an atmosphere where self-confidence and purpose can thrive. She has a strong belief that her role as a parent is not to limit her children's abilities and dreams to make life more convenient for her, but to make adjustments in her life that will incorporate her children and create opportunities for them.

With that vision in mind, Rhonda founded two educational programs: Camp Xander-Well and F.O.C.U.S. (Forget outside Circumstances until Success) Academy. Both programs strive to enhance the educational experience by fostering a love for learning created from an atmosphere conducive to multiple learning styles. Rhonda desires for all children to realize the greatness within themselves. Motivated and inspired by her love for hosting, organizing, and planning events, Rhonda founded, A Genie in a Bottle

Rhonda Bennett

Events, an event planning company that hosts an array of events from weddings and baby showers, to holiday events and various galas.

Rhonda's favorite moments are with her family; whether it's pizza and movie night with her boys, Sunday dinner with close friends, or date night with her hubby, Kevin.

Made in the USA
Charleston, SC
10 April 2015